Trumpty Dumpty 2

From Mother Goose
to Wonderland...

Also by Michael Luzzi

Trumpty Dumpty Invades Mother Goose

(Originally published as Trumpty Dumpty)

Praise for Trumpty Dumpty ...

★★★★★ Amazon Reviewer

Trumpty rhymes full of unbridled candor and hilarity
"Michael Luzzi's rhymes capture the absurdity of the Trump administration with unbridled candor and hilarity. The writer's choice of nursery rhymes as a format for this parody seems eminently appropriate. They echo the jostling, name-calling, impulsive outbursts and gamesmanship of the White House as if they were taking place on a noisy playground.

★★★★ Amazon Reviewer

Nursery Rhyme Serves as Balm and Bomb!!
In seamless prose, Luzzi puts into print all the absurdities of a difficult time in US history, and much like the original Humpty Dumpty, leads us to muse on our limitations to fathom the unfathomable. Hurray for this timely tome! Helps me to keep a sense of balance, and tickles my funny bone. I am grateful for the chuckles and the superb illustrations. Have recommended it to all my friends!

★★★★★ Amazon Reviewer

If it wasn't so funny you would cry.
"This is so funny! If the USA wasn't such a mess thanks to the little person in charge I could laugh forever. Too bad the entire globe no longer looks at America the way it use too (sic), he has changed our view."

Trumpty Dumpty 2
From Mother Goose
to Wonderland...

Michael S. Luzzi

BOGGS HILL BOYS PRESS
173 Boggs Hill Road
Newtown, CT 06470

Front and back cover illustration by John Alderfer
Front and back cover design and interior layout by
Lee Gorman
Author photo by Cornelia Luzzi

Library of Congress Cataloging-in-Publication Data is avail-
able: ISBN -9781732128316

Printed in the United States of America

Dedication

This book is dedicated to Dennis Frusciano, my oldest, dearest mate, with whom I was joined at the hip through elementary school, high school, and beyond, and from whom I learned about the essence of poetry, the value of humor, and the ways of the world in general. It was largely because of Dennis that I became a writer. For the last too many years, we were separated by too many miles to lift a glass together, but the distance took nothing away from the love and the memories. Fruscy, you will always be my brother both on and off the athletic fields where, together, we learned about becoming men. *(6/1/46 – 12/11/19)*

This book is dedicated to Peter Holskin, who welcomed me back to teaching in 2005, and for whom I am grateful for the confidence he instilled in me not only in the classroom but also in the real world. When I was cynical and questioning my worth, Peter always made me feel larger than the life I was struggling with. He was one of the most intelligent, accomplished, compassionate and humble men I have ever known. An unconditional loving friend and mentor. His final words to me: "You're a lucky man." Always in my corner. Petey, may your spirit continue to inhabit me on my never-ending journey to becoming an adult. *(1/10/49 – 1/10/20)*

Table of Contents

Introduction   11

Trumpderland *(Trumpty Dumpty Rhymes)*   13

Classic Poem Parodies   21

Hit Song Parodies   37

The Orange King *(Limericks)*   45

Haiku-ish   55

Good Riddance To You via *(Good Morning To You)* 58

The Fight Goes On *(Late Night Parodies)*   61

Do-It-Yourself *(DIY Limerick Completions)*   71

Do-It-Yourself *(DIY Poem Completions)*   75

Trumpty Dumpty Retrospective   82

Acknowledgements   83

Cover Legend *(Cover Character IDs)*   86-87

"...Mere anarchy is loosed upon the world,
The blood-dimmed tide is loosed, and everywhere
The ceremony of innocence is drowned;
The best lack all conviction, while the worst
Are full of passionate intensity."

From the poem
"The Second Coming"
by William Butler Yeats

Introduction

Why write a second book about the same subject, which I have covered in my first book? Because, "There are more things in heaven and earth, Horatio, Than are dreamt of in your philosophy." (*Hamlet* **(1.5.167-8), Hamlet to Horatio)**.

In my first book, (retitled) *Trumpty Dumpty Invades Mother Goose,* I used well-known characters from nursery rhymes to lampoon real people in Trump's campaign and cabinet. Since then, the frustration after one year has morphed into full-blown incredulity from enduring over three-and-a-half years in this "alternate universe."

I refused to retreat into cynicism and avoided a lapse into glumness. Sarcasm was also out of the question. Such derision and mockery are the tools of the mean-spirited, the cruel, and the unimaginative.

COVID-19 has added a dimension of loneliness to the alienation of almost everyone. The pandemic has widened the divisions in America rather than united us against a common threat. Trump's failed leadership has magnified its impact.

In *Trumpty Dumpty 2 From Mother Goose To Wonderland...,* I have followed POTUS and his associates down the rabbit hole, so to speak. The players in this cast seem more fake and less believable than their Wonderland counterparts. The tools in my repertoire turn out to be variations of poetry: Trumpty Dumpty rhymes, Haiku, original limericks, parodies of classic poems and popular hit songs, and a paean to the Late Night stalwarts I've even included a DIY section for readers to be creative, vent, and have some collective fun. Peace... MSL

"Trumpderland"

The Trumpty Dumpty Rhymes

TRUMPTY DUMPTY used Mother Goose
But I let that parody loose
All the characters from all of those rhymes
Have been sent to safety from Trumpty times

But Trumpty Dumpty has remained
We still have yet to end his reign
Limericks, Haiku, parodies of poems,
All with the intention of sending him home

I've called upon these different forms
Trumpty's antics are far from norms
I will write and fight through November 3rd
To remove Trumpty and his hateful herd

Trumpty Dumpty had settled in
The West Wing filled with kith and kin
Ivanka and Jared there to advise
And Stephen Miller, Minister of Lies

Trumpty Dumpty: Jared Kushner
Trumpty's dark agenda pusher
His job description: Aggravation
As Minister of Misinformation

Trumpty said, "I'll hire the best!"
Really? Trumpty surely you jest.
What are they best at? Doing your bidding?
Say otherwise and we 'll know you're kidding

Trumpty Dumpty wondered why
How'd he ever became this guy
How could those ignorant voters not know
This would become a reality show?

Trumpty Dumpty speaks to his base
Between their ears nothing but space
They repeat his tweets, no matter how vile
We wonder how they will act at his trial

Trumpty Dumpty surely scorned us
Although he did try to warn us
He said he'd build a wall on the border
He took the oath, then he gave the order

Trumpty Dumpty: The Supreme Court
For him it was like a contact sport
When Trumpty nominated Kavanaugh
Hearings were a battlefield; nerves rubbed raw

Trumpty Dumpty briefed on NATO
Said he knew all there was to know
Allies pay too little, it makes no sense
That bases exist just for their defense

Trumpty Dumpty: The NSA
"John Bolton will do what I say."
But there were times they went head to head
And Bolton wrote down everything he said

Trumpty's friends finished a pipeline
Their credo is "What's yours is mine"
Native Americans honored their dead
Modern greed merchants want oil instead

Trumpty Dumpty – the past three years
Re-enacted the "Trail of Tears"
For Immigration there's a solution
He'll just nullify the Constitution

Trumpty Dumpty three years later
Both Chief Tweeter and Chief Hater
All the world's leaders their efforts combined
Couldn't get Trumpty to learn to be kind

Trumpty Dumpty thinks he's a king
Wants everyone to kiss his ring
Trumpty bought jewels to display on his band
Made the ring too big for his little hand

Trumpty poisoned the GOP
Making it "The Party of Me"
And his Senate lackeys just jumped on board
And just like Trumpty, they're out of their gourd

Trumpty and Reagan both leaned right
But Trumpty isn't very bright
Reagan was kind, treated Tip with humor
Trump tweets venom, not only for Schumer

Trumpty's lawyer, Michael Cohen
Had a whistle started blowin'
Trumpty is ruthless; it's time to come clean
Liar, cheater, fraud – you know what I mean

Trumpty Dumpty: The Covid Virus
Trumpty said it would go by us
Called it a hoax, said we've got it controlled
American lives have since been on hold

Trumpty Dumpty: Covid-19
Pandemic like we've never seen
All the physicians and scientists too
Tried to tell Trumpty it wasn't the flu

Trumpty Dumpty: Black Lives Matter
To him it's just idle chatter
What's he to do? He couldn't stay quiet
Needs militant! Called protests a "riot".

Trumpty Dumpty needed a prop
Trumpty wanted a photo op
Something dramatic, something viable:
In front of a church…holding a bible

Trumpty Dumpty loved the notion
Trumpty's goons put plans in motion
We'll use noxious fumes and rubber pellets
To disperse the crowd of peaceful zealots

Lafayette Square like a war zone
Couldn't leave well enough alone
It was dangerous, they had to use force
Hey, had to keep POTUS safe of course

There he stood in front of the church
Trumpty should have done some research
Instead he held the bible upside down
He looked (if possible) more like a clown

Trumpty says his life matters, too
(But not the same as me and you)
It's like he *tries*... to make people abhor him
Because he's POTUS we can't ignore him

Trumpty says he believes in God...
Does anyone else find this odd?
I mean – he held the bible upside down!
(I wonder if God believes in this clown?)

At the White House protests outside
Trumpty Dumpty said, "I must hide!
Get me to the bunker and build a fence;
Prepare my toupee and makeup for Pence"

Secret Service exchanged a look
Had to get Trumpty off the hook
That Pence ploy won't work, the detail noted
Mike's thin as a rail; Trumpty is...bloated

Trumpty Dumpty became enraged,
Insisted the body double be staged
"Sir, the protesters will see through the ruse,
Say Trumpty's just making another excuse

"Trumpty's a coward," they'll all say;
"He proves it many times each day."
"Call FOX," said Trumpty ..."I'll need protection
Say I'm only doing an inspection"

Trumpty Dumpty: Issue du jour
Another pile of horse manure
The Senate and Fake News all took the bait
Get to the bottom of "Obamagate"

Trumpty:"World's most dangerous man"
Says niece Mary, despite the ban
Her memoir,"Too Much and Never Enough"
A book filled with Trumpty's personal stuff

Trumpty Dumpty watched his TV
Donald watched Joe name his VP
All the media: Fake News and FOX too
Agree Kamala was a major coup

Classic Poem Parodies

With gratitude & apologies to:

Maya Angelou
Robert Burns
Robert Frost
A.E. Housman
Langston Hughes
Edgar Allan Poe
Edwin Arlington Robinson
Ernest Lawrence Thayer
William Butler Yeats

"To A Deadbeat's Lying Tongue" *via "To An Athlete Dying Young"* *

That time, the Presidential race
We wish that you'd won second place;
Man and boy stood weeping by,
And women wondered why-oh-why?

Today, the swamp all liars swum
With bold strokes, not just playing dumb,
And voters set the threshold low
Not knowing what they didn't know.

Slick man who hoodwinked many fools
To trust him, then be used like tools,
And early though the lies were bought
They withered quicker than you thought

Eyes that the falsehoods deftly shut
Can finally see just what is what
As shouts of protest fall on you
Prepare, at last, to get your due

Now, you will not strut and swagger
As voters wield a deadly dagger
Cutting short your dangerous reign
Of breaking laws, inflicting pain

In place of two terms and a crown
A failed monarch…instead, a clown
And as the sweat drips from your wig
We the people will dance a jig

*Poem * "To an Athlete Dying Young" by A.E. Housman*

"Liar and Race" *via "Fire and Ice"**

Some say the world will end with a Liar
Some say with Race
From what I've seen of Trump's Empire
I hold with those who favor the Liar
But if someone were to make the case
I think I know enough of hate
To say that for destruction Race
Is also the perfect bait
To cause the fall from Grace

* Poem "Fire and Ice" by Robert Frost

"When You Are Odd" *via "When You Are Old"**

When you are odd and bald and full of fat
And nodding by the TV,
Take down this book
Slowly turn pages, give pictures that look
Your eyes once had, as if to say, "What's that?"

How many spurned your moments of sad shame
And loathed your phony wig and orange hue
But one man loved the darkened soul of you
And who was that man?
Good ol' what's-his-name!

And bending down in the glow of Fox News
Murmur low, how I'm glad it was me
Who had become the party's nominee
Instead of that incompetent Ted Cruz

* Poem "When You are Old" by William Butler Yeats 23

"Still That Guy" *via "Still I Rise"* *

We will write you down in history
With your appetite for pie.
You may want to send us to the swamp;
But still you'll be that guy.

Does our irreverence upset you?
Why are you obsessed with hate?
'Cause we know that we've got facts and truth
Piling high upon our plate.

Just like moons and like suns,
With the certainty you'll lie.
Just like no hope that you will change,
You still lie,
You're still that guy.

Do you want to see us broken?
Shoulders hunched and mournful sighs?
Not a chance for that to happen,
We'll lift our heads up to the skies.

Does our haughtiness offend you?
Don't say. We all know why
'Cause you've no idea what haughty means,
Sadly, you're still that guy.

You may shoot us with your "best words",
You may glare with raccoon eyes,
You may pretend that you are smart,
But, still you lie
Does our morality upset you?

Well, we've got a full supply.
Why are we aloof, you want some proof?
The proof is you're that guy.

Out of the huts of history's shame
You lie
 Up from a past where you're to blame
You lie
We're all immigrants black, brown, and white,
Swelling with pride, bathed in bright light.
Leaving behind your tragic flaw
You lie
Into a land with rule of law
You're *not that* guy
Bearing the lessons our ancestors gave,
In the "land of the free and home of the brave"
But, still you lie
You lie
You lie
You're still that guy.

* *Poem "Still I Rise" by Maya Angelou*

"A Blue, Blue Day" *via* "A Red, Red Rose" *

O my scorn is like a blue, blue day
Echoes of November;
O my scorn is like a mournful dirge
Each time I remember.

So foul art thou, oh wretched one,
So deep am I in a funk;
Our nation needs a miracle
To rise from where we've sunk.

To rise from where we've sunk with you,
Who's led us down the Rabbit Hole;
Our nation needs a miracle
To once again reclaim its soul.

I hope you pay, my bogus liege!
A consequence without delay;
And take that orange mug of yours
And rue your blue, blue day.

* Poem "A Red, Red Rose" by Robert Burns

"Senate" *via "Harlem"**

What happens to an Impeachment deferred?

Does it dry up
like an injustice that's been done?
Or fester in the Senate–
Until the next one?
Does it reek like a stagnant swamp?
Swarming with wrinkly white men?
Or stick in the craw–
like a perversion of law?

Maybe it just fades
like it doesn't matter.

Or does it shatter?

* Poem "Harlem" by Langston Hughes

"Minihands Skeevy" *via "Miniver Cheevy"**

Minihands Skeevy, child of scorn,
   Grew fat while he abused his powers;
We wept that he was ever born,
   And built Trump Towers.

Minihands loved his previous life
   When he conned folks and took their money;
Melania may be his wife
   She's not his honey.

Minihands sighed for what he missed
   And dreamed of having bigger fingers;
For tiny hands, he had been dissed…
   Resentment lingers.

Minihands mourned his lowly status
   That discerning people despised him;
He mourned the spreading of his fat ass
   His girth belied him.

Minihands loved McD's Double Cheese;
   The fact is he ate one every night
While watching Fox on three TVs,
   A pathetic sight.

Minihands cursed his White House digs
   And longed for gold-plated toilet bowls;
He claimed the place was fit for pigs,
   But not for tweeting trolls.

Minihands scorned the office he held
   And his vile ways abused it;
We all wish he would feel impelled
   Not to use it.

Minihands Skeevy, born too late,
   Rubbed his stomach and kept repeating:
"Up" is Down and "Love" is Hate,"
   And kept on eating.

Poem "Miniver Cheevy" by Edwin Arlington Robinson

"Stopping For Food On A Snowy Evening"
via "Stopping By Woods..." *

Whose meal this is I think I know
His house is in Mar-a-logo
He will not see me stopping here
To watch him binge on pizza dough

My companions must think it queer
Of all places, I should stop here
Between Palm Beach and Southern Bridge
With Secret Service very near

They give their heads a perplexed shake
As if I'd made some grave mistake
The only other sound's unspoken
Trumpty chewing with his mouth open

Sneaking a glimpse, so rare indeed
Catch the "smartest" president feed
His face with – yep – the fastest speed
Symbolic of his tremendous greed
Symbolic of his tremendous greed

* Poem "Stopping by Woods on a Snowy Evening" by Robert Frost

"TrumptyBellee" *via "Annabel Lee"* *

It was not so many years ago
At a golf club by the sea
That a con man there lived whom you may know
By the name of Trumpty Dumpty
And this scam artist lived with no other thought
Than to dupe and swindle you and me

We were not children, *he* was the child
In his playpen by the sea
And there was no love lost, none-zero-zip
Between Trumpty and you and me
With his toddler-tantrums and hateful tweets
Love lost… How could there be?!

And this was one reason not long ago
At (Sub) Par-A-Lago by the sea
Dark clouds gathered, thick with resentment
As he approached the first tee

Loud foul air escaped from his hind parts – choking
The electorate – you and me
So the Secret Service arrived with facemasks
Thank God they heard our plea

They rushed him to his odor-proof bunker
In his playroom by the sea
And there he remained tweeting excuses and blame
Hugging his Fox TV
Waiting for Hannity

* Poem "Annabel Lee " by Edgar Allan Poe

"Richman Gory" *(aka Trumpty Dumpty) via*
*"Richard Cory"**

Whenever Trumpty Dumpty gave a speech
We people watching TV looked away
He was guaranteed to make some breach
Of truth in anything he had to say

And he always wore ties that were too long
And always illiterate when he spoke
As we perceived him – anything but strong
The fact is we considered him a joke

And he was rich? Hm-m... how would we know?
And his school records were a mystery
In truth, his level of knowledge was low
(We wish he knew more about history)

So on we worked; at night we knelt to pray
That the electorate would remember
How "mean" and "nasty" Trump's tweets were each day
And put an end to him in November

*Poem "Richard Cory" by Edwin Arlington Robinson

"Ballad of the Trumplord" *via "Ballad of the Landlord"* *

Trumpty, Trumplord,
Our nation's sprung a leak
Don't you remember your promise
To care for our weak?

Trumpty, Trumplord,
The system's broken down
You can see for yourself those in need
Are mostly black and brown

The taxes you say we owe you
According to what we earn
We'll gladly pay you that and more
When you show us your return

What? You target illegals at the border?
You can't tell one from the other?
Yet you round them up in cages
Separating a child from its mother.

Um-huh! You talk high and mighty
Though most of what you say's absurd
Your blathering won't mean too much
After your reckoning on November 3rd

Police! Police!
Go and arrest these protesters
They're challenging our government
With their peaceful gestures

Shields and nightsticks!
Tear gas! Subdue.

Military tactics.
Unmarked vans.
Headlines in fake news:
BLM THREATENS TRUMPLORD
RIOTS DOOMED TO FAIL.
LAWLESSNESS SENDS ANTIFA
TO ROT IN UNKNOWN JAIL.

·Poem *"Ballad of the Landlord"* by Langston Hughes

"Trumpty at the Tee" *via "Casey at the Bat"**

It looked extremely rocky for the White House Four that day;
Trumpty's group was down by one with a single hole to play.
And when Miller sliced his drive, and Mnuchin did the same,
Spectators began to speculate about whom Trumpty would blame.

Some diehard fans paced back and forth and wondered what came next.
Some crossed their fingers, others prayed, and more began to text;
They thought if Trump could just man up and maybe reach the green–
The match might still be winnable and thus avoid a scene.

But Barr preceded Trumpty (since he had replaced Mike Pence);
The VP became Trump's caddy, which made a lot more sense.
The AG's pace, that look on his face… no one made a sound;
A deathlike silence gripped the crowd; Barr didn't mess around.

He whacked the cover off the ball, grunting all the while;
Trumpty's choice for head of justice, he liked his macho style.
As the broken ball descended, all strained to watch it land;
Trumpty wrung his tiny hands as it settled in the sand.

And Biden's team was on it, and Joe was tough in the clutch;
And Mueller's drive was mighty! Did he have the magic touch?
But Schiff's shot hooked, it didn't look as if he could hold par,
And Trump didn't doubt it would all work out; it had so far…

From the partisan multitude, up went a joyous yell;
Like the roar at Trumpty's rallies, it took some time to quell.
The tourney was at Bedminster, Trumpty's home turf, of course;
Biden's team stood by patiently until the crowd went hoarse.

There was tension in his checkered pants holding up his gut.
(Sometimes he had to suck it in or couldn't see his putt).
But he played so much golf here he was confident and knew
His practiced drive would yield him a great putting line in two.

There was ease in Trumpty's manner as he stepped up to the tee;
Pride in his face, his wig in place, so freakin' smug was he;
He waddled, stopped, and then he popped a thumbs up to the crowd;
That's not all… he placed the ball on the tee, then took a bow.

His drive was straight and long and landed almost on the green;
A chip near the cup, another thumbs up: a hopeful scene.
But who could know that he could blow a putt so near the cup?
Like striking out in baseball when you were batting clean up.

Biden's team was Adam Schiff, Bob Mueller, and Obama;
They couldn't resist pumping their fists, shouting, "Yeah, Mama!
"Trumpty looked shocked, so did his flock, then he threw his putter.
It made no sense that he blamed Pence and began to sputter.

While shaming his Veep for failing to keep Trump from this fate,
Joe's foursome began to pour some champagne to celebrate.
POTUS turned his head: Someone said, "Hey, don't blame your caddy."
Trump was shocked! It was Barack who mouthed the words:
"Who's your daddy?"

* Poem, "Casey at the Bat" by Ernest Lawrence Thayer

Hit Song Parodies

With gratitude
& apologies to:

Billy Joel
Carly Simon
Grace Slick

Piano Man* Parody *(2016 ELECTION)*

It's 10 p.m. on Election Night,
It looks like Trump's going to win,
There's a bunch of folks standing next to me
In this moment we've all become kin

They say, "Son can you play us a memory
We're not really sure how it goes
But it's sad, now not sweet, and a bitter defeat
By a fool that so few people chose."

La la la, di da da La la, di da da da dum

Chorus:
Sing us a song, you're the piano man
Give us some hope tonight
'Cause we all feel the need for a parody
To help us get feeling alright

Now, this candidate isn't a friend of mine
Though Trump seems to think he might be
And he's quick with a tweet but let me repeat
I have chosen to vote Hillary
He said, "Bill I believed in your compliment –
'Entertainer' – you sang me that song;
Well, I know you want me as president,"
(He couldn't be any more wrong!)

Oh, la la la, di da da La la, di da da da dum

Now Don is a real estate broker
Who's had time to marry three wives

And he's tweeting that Clinton, has done what
she didn't And he piles more lies onto lies

And his campaign is practicing dirty tricks
As they met with the Russians for sure
Yes they're sharing secrets called politics
But it smells a lot more like manure

Chorus:
Sing us a song, you're the piano man
Give us some hope tonight
'Cause we all feel the need for a parody
To help us get feeling alright

It's a pretty poor turnout by voters
The electorate should be ashamed
'Cause they don't realize that a fool in disguise
Will be changing the rules of the game
And my song starts to sound like a eulogy
And the atmosphere starts smelling stale
And they stand there dejected by who got elected
And cry out, "Lord, where have we failed?"

Oh, la la la, di da da La la, di da da da dum

Chorus:
Sing us a song, you're the piano man
Give us some hope tonight
'Cause we all feel the need for a parody
To help us get feeling alright

* Based on the song "Piano Man" by Billy Joel

Piano Man* Parody *(2016 AFTERMATH)*

It's anytime and it's every day
The Tweets appear in the news
A Trump advisor waits in the wings
Ready to counter these views

Tweet says, "All going well at the White House,
Believe me, everything's fine."
But the verdict is in, and not even his kin,
Can deny that he's out of his mind.

La la la, di da da La la, di da da da dum

Chorus:
Sing us a song, you're the piano man
Please give it to us straight
Tell us how to remove him from office
How much longer do we have to wait

Now Sean at the podium was a joke
It was easy for all to see,
He was quick to deny, say he didn't know why?
But there's someplace that he'd rather be
He said, "Why the hell am I doing this?"
With a quizzical look on his face
"Well I'm sure I'd respond to de-programming
If I could get out of this place."

Oh, la la la, di da da La la, di da da da dum

Now Kushner's the president's son-in-law
Ivanka is his lovely wife

And his Faustian pact still remains intact
And probably will be for life

And the Cabinet practice allegiance
As the nation goes down the drain
Yes, they're sharing a rite called obeisance
Which we all know is wholly insane

Chorus:
Sing us a song, you're the piano man
Please give it to us straight
Tell us how to remove him from office
How much longer do we have to wait

It's a pretty sad time for America
For most folks it's like a bad dream
Scaramucci's the most recent casualty
For which there's no adequate meme
And the patience around the world's waning
Fearing nuclear war's on the brink
We're all holding our breath, trying to cheat
death
Praying, "Please let Trump's fascist ship sink!"

Oh, la la la, di da da La la, di da da da dum

Chorus:
Sing us a song, you're the piano man
Please give it to us straight
Tell us how to remove him from office
How much longer do we have to wait?

Based on the song 'Piano Man" by Billy Joel

"Dag Nabbit" *via "White Rabbit"**

One lie makes you angry
And one sticks in your craw
And the ones that Trumpty gives you
Are as phony as his wall
Don't ask Clinton
She's not on call

And if Trumpty chases porn stars
And he knows he breaks the law
Tell him a Putin-looking caterpillar
Has given him a call
He called Clinton
And that's not all

When white men in the Senate
Rise in lock step then you know
They've killed bills for vets and seniors
They're fake, fraudulent and faux
 Don't call Clinton
 Just vote for Joe

When logic and proportion
Are declared legally dead
And The White Knight looks like Jared
And The Queen's got Melania's head
Remember, Cohen's dormouse said:
Heed your head
Heed your head

* Based on the song, "White Rabbit" by Grace Slick (Jefferson Airplane Surrealistic Pillow album 1967)

"You're So Lame" *via "You're So Vain"**

You limped into the White House
Like you were shuffling down a ramp
Your hair strategically glued above both eyes
You looked like an orange lamp
You had both hands on your water glass
So your shirt wouldn't get damp
And all your staff walked on egg shells
Staff walked on egg shells, and...

You're so lame,
You probably think you're a stable genius
You're so lame (you're so lame)
I'll bet you're thinking stable genius
Don't you?
Don't you?

You conned the voters 4 years ago
When they thought that you were sane
Well you said that you were the only one
To make America great again
But you gave away false (high?) hopes and
dreams
And left us all in pain
We had some dreams – became nightmares
about you
Nightmares about you, and

You're so lame,
You probably think this verse is a tribute
You're so lame (so lame)
I'll bet you think this verse is a tribute
Don't you?
Don't you?
Don't you?

Well I hear you went down to Mar-a-Lago
And cheated at golf and won
Then you looked straight up, no protective eyewear
To see the total eclipse of the sun
Well, you're where you should be most of the time
And when you're not, you're with a yuge
abundance of fast food
In bed watching TV
In bed watching TV, and...

You're so lame,
You probably think you fooled us forever
You're so lame (so lame)
I'll bet you think you fooled us forever
Don't you?
Don't you?
Don't you?

You're so lame,
So far from a stable genius
You're so lame,
I'll bet you think you're smarter than Jesus
You're so vain

* Based on the song, "You're So Vain" by Carly Simon, 1971.

"The Orange King"

The Limericks

Including:
the characters from the
cover... all inhabitants of
Trumpderland

Some people have questioned my motives
For writing a book so explosive
Well, the list is too long
About all that is wrong
With Trumpty…He's much too corrosive

A "Rabbit Hole" leads to the unknown
Could be a danger to go alone
But the population
Of the Trumpty Nation
Led the way into this Twilight Zone

Like Alice followed the White Rabbit
Backing Trumpty became a habit
They followed him blindly
Way out of his mind, he
Inspired me to write, "Dag Nabbit

Trumpty's a liar extraordinaire
But Vlad steered us from "buyer beware"
The votes were collected
Hackers were detected
Stench of Putin's blackmail in the air

The Caterpillar looks on from above
Eyes on Trumpty but no look of love
Always near his hookah
Henceforth, Putin-ookah
New U.S website: Putin.gov

There once was a press secretary
Whose disposition was contrary
Wait! There was more than one
For Trumpty's will to be done
Their similar approach was scary

First Sean, Then Sarah, now Kayleigh
A straight answer – never...or maybe?
Who had the best style
For constant denial
To the Press Corps we ask, "What say ye?"

Impossible to omit Conway
Kellyanne would not be kept at bay
Call her on an issue
She'll dig in and diss you
There's no way she's not having her say

Take the protests at Lafayette Park
She declared (with her usual snark)
There were riots of course
So they had to use force
Or else Trumpty would never embark

What can you say about William Barr?
Attorney General? Har-Har-Har!
Top lawyer in the land
Puts his head in the sand
When Trumpty's behavior goes too far

John Bolton had many detractors
His hawkishness one of the factors
But his revealing book
Gives an intimate look
At Trumpty and all his contractors

Need a full page devoted to Mitch
A real master of "bait and switch"
Pitched us Democracy
Sold us Autocracy
He can't tell (but we know) which is which

And Mitch had it out for Obama
Went after him like a piranha
Blocked all legislation
That might help the nation
That traitor turned hate into drama

The Senate Majority Leader
A quintessential Bottom Feeder
Sneaky reptile from Hell
Lurked in his turtle shell
Mitch hissed while Trumpty used his tweeter

The March Hare: See the look on Flynn's face
Makes it appear he feels out of place
Did he show up tardy?
No, not at this party
It's about jail without bail, his disgrace.

Mad Hatter is a codger named Roger
Who's behaved like the Artful Dodger
Though Stone is far from dumb
We hope that he'll become
In prison – a permanent lodger

U.S. Treasurer as Cheshire Cat
Let's see…What's more ironic than that?
Like to wipe that smug grin
From his chinny-chin-chin
Mnuchin hitting floor with a splat

Trumpty has Graham constantly lying
On the cover Lindsay is crying
Babes cry when they're tired
Are these tears inspired
By the Senator's career dying

The Walrus and Carpenter – Behold!
Rudy and Chris are comedic gold
The Laurel and Hardy
Of the Grand Ol' Party
Part of the flock, they do what they're told

Trumpty Dumpty can always rely
On these two because they always try
To be in his good grace
Even if they lose face
Like their fictional brethren, that's why

The Queen sees croquet as a thriller
Her Flamingo Mallet is Miller
A proponent of hate
See his face! He can't wait
To make every player a killer

The Lizard, the Duchess, the Dodo
Manafort, Devos, and Pompeo
Lizard – ineffective
Duchess – quite defective
And Dodo taught Trumpty Quid Pro Quo

Eric is the Queen's Rook, Tweedle Dee
Which makes sense, a mama's boy is he
Jr. had to succumb
To being Tweedle Dum
And the King's Rook, the fall guy for Trump

Tweedle Dum – Trumpty's first son, nee Don
Thought he had to answer to no one
For lies about the masks
He was taken to task
'Twas Tweeter Dumb, now he's Twitter Done!

There once was a (fill in the blank?) named
Hannity
Like Trumpty, full of false vanity
No matter who he mocks
His loyal sheep at Fox
Hang on his words…It's insanity!

Mount Rushmore residents heard the news
Four presidents who had paid their dues
Honored for their service
Even *they* became nervous
What if this wasn't a Trumpty Ruse?

They called an emergency meeting
There'd never been any competing
No "most" "best" or "greatest"
Or "hate" "hater" "hatest"
And, most of all, no freakin' tweeting

So, Trumpty wants to be on Rushmore
Well, let's see what he is best known for:
Highest trade deficit
Adding trillions to debt
Leading Putin right to our front door

The takeaway: Trumpty went to see
The tribute to the Presidency
POTUS eyed Mt. Rushmore
Then just glared at the four
Scoffed, then grumbled, "Why isn't it me?"

Tune into a Trumpty interview
Try to figure out what you would do
If you had to sit down
Across from this clown
And make sense of his warped point of view

He sits with an arsenal of lies
Not even an attempt to disguise
What he knows is nonsense
No hint of recompense
And says he deserves a Nobel Prize

Never been a Commander-in-Chief
Who behaved worse than a common thief
But no one could compare
To the man who's now there
He's gotta go! We need some relief…

Dr. Fauci has received death threats
But Trumpty's silence aids and abets
His main lunatic fringe
When they become unhinged
POTUS is master; they're just puppets

If Trumpty would get off the couch, he
Could address the threats against Fauci
He could respond instead
Of burying his head
In his default position: Grouchy

The niece of our recent president
Appalled by this White House resident
Said she had to speak out
To erase any doubt
For him no truths are self-evident

A shout out to Trumpty's niece, Mary
Whose book revelations were scary
Said, "Enough is enough!"
And exposed Trumpty's bluff
Despite our despair, "Thanks for sharing"

Trump seemed to feel he should be a Tsar
Bolton noticed that on his radar
Thought, No! What could be worse
Than Tsar Trumpty the First?
(So) Bolton wrote A White House Memoir

On the cover The Gryphon, Bill Barr
(His appearance is rather bizarre)
With Mitch he seems cozy
Where do you suppose he
And the turtle believe that they are?

Eagerly awaiting Cohen's book
Another revealing inside look
The title is fitting
And very hard hitting
Disloyal won't let Trump off the hook!

Joe picked Kamala to be his Veep
Biden had made a promise to keep
He said, "Wait, you will see
That my choice for VP:
An overdue political leap"

Trumpty team went into defense mode
Did Biden hit the Mother Lode?
POTUS met with the Press
Couldn't conceal his stress
Like his head was about to explode!

The Racist-in-Chief had beans to spill
Reprised his role as a Birther shill
First it was Obama
And now it's Kamala
This president has too much time to kill

Trumpty is like a human tumor
Pick a host site; he'll grow a rumor
The man is too broken
A pathetic token:
Fake Person with no sense of humor

An issue that needs to gain traction
Get rid of political factions
Neither party makes sense
Always on the offense
This country needs a call to action

Haiku – ish

If no one were there
When Trump fell in the forest
Would ~~there be a sound~~ anyone care?

Man walks into a bar
Waits for election outcome
If Trump wins, he stays

How much is enough?
How often has this been said?
Not often enough!

Senators take oaths
Citizens take leaps of faith
They pass in the night

Trumpty's election
Shined a spotlight on the world
Then the stage went dark

 Long before Covid
The world faced another threat:
The Trumpty Pandemic

"Nothing Gold Can Stay"
Why did Frost choose that color?
He shoulda said "Orange"

See, Dick. See Trumpty's staff.
See them come and see them go
See Jane blink. They're gone *

Down the Rabbit Hole
So many went willingly
Now looking for the light

"Ignorance is bliss"
Not a common phrase for kids
For voters: Tragic

Joe and Kamala
BIDEN and HARRIS: Our hope…
Make America Matter
(Again)

November The Third
What an opportunity
To make history

*See **"Good Riddance To You"** parody verse via "Good
Morning To You"*

Good Riddance To You *via Good Morning To*
You (Trumpty's Cabinet 3 Years Later)

Good riddance to you,
Good riddance to you,
You all took your places
With grins on your faces
Rich, greedy and white
But not very bright
Good riddance, we're so glad you're gone
(We've had quite enough of your con…)

Good riddance to you,
Good riddance to you,
Tom Price picked for Health Care
But cheated on airfare
You played to Trump's base
"Repeal and replace"
Good riddance to you in this poem
(A chartered flight will take you home…)

Good riddance to you,
Good riddance to you,
Ah, Little Jeff Sessions
We'll give our impressions:
You got what was due
Trump never liked you
Good riddance, you racist AG
(Hope you don't get out of jail free…)

Good riddance to you,
Good riddance to you,
You sycophant Priebus
Tried hard to deceive us
But too bad that Trump
Played you for a chump
Good riddance, Herr first Chief of Staff
(No secret that you'd get the shaft...)

Good riddance to you,
Good riddance to you,
Advisor Steve Bannon
Trump's resident Klansman
The havoc you wreaked
With all that you leaked
Good riddance, so glad you were fired
(Your absence has made us inspired...)

Good riddance to you,
Good riddance to you,
It couldn't feel nicer
To say bye to Spicer
He fed us the news
With verbal abuse
Good riddance, tough luck for you, Sean
(Too bad, but we're glad that you're gone...)

Good riddance to you,
Good riddance to you,
There went Michael Cohen
With all that he's knowin'
Could do Trumpty harm
He tripped an alarm
Good riddance, your info makes sense
(Have you any dirt on Mike Pence?...)

Good riddance to you,
Good riddance to you,
Brave General Kelly
We know that your belly
Got filled with Trump's waste
But you're not disgraced
Good riddance, you gave it your best
(No one – even you – could have guessed...)

Good riddance to you,
Good riddance to you,
Mad Dog, Gen'ral Mattis
We know that you had us
In mind to be saved
From one so depraved
Good riddance, thanks for your service
(You tried, but we're all still nervous...)

Good riddance all you,
Good riddance all you,
For all the excitement
You're under indictment
You all broke the law
You thought no one saw
Good riddance, you played fast and loose
(But really pissed off Mother Goose...)

Late Night Parodies

The Fight Goes On

Trumpty: Late Night Devotee

Trumpty Dumpty, caught in a trap,
Late-night liberals causing a flap,
Colbert, Noah, Kimmel, Meyers, and Maher,
Samantha, and Oliver…They go too far!

All of those snowflakes cross the line,
White House needs to give them a sign-
Call the FCC and the NIA,
You're president, so make them go away

Trumpty, what's your apprehension?
How's that?…you like the attention!?
The mocking accusations – they're all true??
Worst case scenario: That's *really* you!

Trumpty Dumpty: Heir Apparent

Trumpty Dumpty: Screw Bill Maher,
He always takes his jokes too far;
If you can't beat 'em, sue 'em's what I say.
Sir, you've already sued Maher; did he pay?

Trumpty Dumpty probed Obama,
Then Maher questioned Trump's real mama;
Each week Maher baited him with this harangue:
"Prove that she wasn't an orangutan!"

Maher showed an ape's pic side-by-side
With Trump's claiming hair was bonafide
Proof that Donald coulda been sired
By one with hair as orange as fire.

Baa Baa, Bill Maher

Baa-Baa, Bill Maher,
Have you some "New Rules"?
Of course, given the sources sir,
No shortage of new fools.

Some for the public,
Severely dumbed down;
Some for the media
Who act like clowns;
Some for celebrities – royalty? Not!
Some for opponents of legalizing pot.

Baa-baa, Bill Maher,
Have you some New Rules?
Yes, sir, the best for Politico tools.

Where Have You Been, Trevor Noah?
via Billy Boy

Oh where have you been,
Trevor No-, Trevor No-,
Oh where have you been,
Trevor Noah?
Many years I had to hide
You know, given Apartheid
I was young then
And could not leave my mother

Did she make you follow rules,
Trevor No-, Trevor No-,
Was she strict about those rules,
Trevor Noah?
Not to obey mother's law
Would have been a tragic flaw
You got one chance
And there would be no other.

So, South Africa was hard,
Trevor No-, Trevor No-,
Were you living life in fear,
Trevor Noah?
Yes, to keep me from harm's way
How my mother she did pray
I was light-skinned
And we were judged by color.

But you made it here at last,
Trevor No-, Trevor No-,
Now the U.S. is a home,
Trevor Noah?
Well, Jon Stewart had left his post
I'm The Daily Show's new host
Just like Huck Finn
I finally got my druthers.

Now, I'm sending you my book
Trevor No-, Trevor, No-,
Trumpty Dumpty it is called,
Trevor Noah.
I am loving *Born A Crime,*
Mine's a parody of rhymes
Hope you'll read it
(Then share it with Bob Mueller?)

If that's asking way too much,
Trevor No-, Trevor No-,
I am sorry in advance,
Trevor Noah.
See my life is at a stage
(Just about two times your age)
It's my first book,
There may not be another...

Yes, I thanked you in my book,
Trevor No-, Trevor No-,
You and others from Late Night,
Trevor Noah.
Every night you made me laugh
At the latest Trumpty gaffe,
Wishing White House
Hijinks were so much duller.

And, I wanted to partake
Trevor No-, Trevor No-,
To contribute to the cause
Trevor Noah.
Mother Goose and I had fun
Took eight months to get it done,
Want our great land
To keep from being smothered

So, where have I been
Trevor No-, Trevor No-,
Finding ways to contact you,
Trevor Noah.
If you find you like my book
Ask your fans to take a look
If it's helpful,
I'll work on a whole nother.

Last Week Tonight *via Good Morning To You*
(John Oliver)

Good evening to you,
Good evening to you,
It's *Last Week Tonight* time
A John Oli-ver rhyme
He tries to make sense
Of recent events
Good evening, now sit back, relax
While Oliver presents the facts…

Good evening to you,
Good evening to you,
Now John's pretty pumped up
By news that's been Trumped up
He filters all rumors
Through his lens of humor
Good evening, this won't take too long
For him to dissect what's gone wrong…

Good evening to you,
Good evening to you,
Watch how he exposes
Fools, then rubs their noses
In scams they devised
So please be advised
Good evening, it's too good to miss
Reminders each week to RESIST…

Good evening to you,
Good evening to you,
To prove John's persistence
Let's take a for instance
Like *InfoWars* fool, Alex Jones:
John stripped this buffoon to the bones
Good evening, he cut to the quick
Revealed Jones to be a real (insert word that
rhymes w/dick)

Good evening to you,
Good evening to you,
A *Daily Show* fixture
John's humor, a mixture
Of parody plus
Perverse wit and thus
Good Evening, *Last Week...* is a hit
Bravo, I say, "cheers" to this Brit!

Trumpty Vs. Colbert: The Movie
via Humpty Dumpty

I. Exposition

Trumpty Dumpty: "Stephen Colbert?
That guy doesn't come up for air…"
Nasty monologues, brutal slights,
Bashing the president just can't be right."

"Trumpty Dumpty, what will you do
If Colbert keeps mimicking you?
Impersonate him back! Challenge that nerd!
Make him eat crow; use all your best word (sic)"

II. Rising Action

Trumpty Dumpty puffed, *"I'll be great!"*
"You show him, sir, the world can't wait."
Trumpty grinned at his mirror, *"I'm the best!
I'll put all those tales of dumbness to rest!"*

Trumpty Dumpty sat on his throne,
Decided to practice all on his own.
All the fool's mouthpieces were kept away,
So Big Boy could prepare for his big day.

III. Climax

"Trumpty Dumpty, how did it go?
What happened on the Colbert show?
You tear him a new one? Show him who's who?
Humiliate him with your higher IQ?"

IV. Falling Action

"Trumpty, what? You didn't appear?
Good call, you're smarts are nowhere near
Colbert's; face it, your scam would be exposed;
He'd set you on fire, then be the hose!"

V. Resolution

Trumpty Dumpty, justice be served,
You called out Colbert...you've got nerve!
Maybe? But, intelligence? You've got none;
"No-talent Colbert?" He'd whup you for fun.

Do-It-Yourself (DIY)
Limerick Parodies

DIY Limerick Completion

Classic Limerick Form:

Have fun making up and filling in the missing liens in each limerick...

Lines 1,2 and 5 each has 9 beats with end rhymes (A)
Lines 3 & 4 each has 6 beats with end rhymes (B)

(9) There once was a man from Nantucket (A)
(9) Who kept all his cash in a bucket. (A)
(6) But his daughter, named Nan, (B)
(6) Ran away with a man (B)
(9) And as for the bucket, Nantucket (A)

(1) 9   There once was a president from Queens A
     9   Who never says what he really means A
     6
     6
     9

(2) 9   Senate majority leader, Mitch
     9   Whatever he says comes with a hitch
     6
     6
     9

(3) 9   Why would anyone ever agree
     9   To a high-ranking post for Trumpty
     6
     6
     9

(4) 9 There are rules "According to Hoyle"
     9 Card members agree to be loyal
     6
     6
     9

(5) 9
     9
     6 He was named Chief of Staff
     6 And no one dared to laugh
     9

(6) 9
     9
     6 He made deals with Russia
     6 But were kept hush-husha
     9

(7) 9 There are some thoughts about the campaign
     9 That Trump doesn't want to end his reign
     6
     6
     9

(8) 9
     9
     6 What would be most absurd
     6 On November the 3rd
     9

Do-It-Yourself (DIY) Poem Parodies

With gratitude & apologies to:

William Blake
Anne Bradstreet
Elizabeth Barrett Browning
Rudyard Kipling
Edgar Allan Poe
Dylan Thomas

"The "Braveman" via "The Raven" *

Once upon a TV season, while I pondered
   viewer treason,
Over many a lame and curious failing of the
   network news –
While I flip-flopped, not decidin', suddenly
   there was Joe Biden
Out from hidin', gamely stridin', right inside my
   chamber door
"What the f...," I stated, to the campaign I
   donated all I had –
Only that and nothing more

*Poem **"The Raven"** by Edgar Allan Poe

(Use space below to have some fun continuing the parody)

"Trumpty Trumpster" *via "The Tyger"* *

TrumptyTrumpster burning bright
From the TV screen at night
What tiny hand or bloodshot eye
Could frame thy pre-obesity?

In what distant swamps or sewers
Swam that portly frame of yours
On what wings does he aspire
That wouldn't land him in the mire

* Poem **"The Tyger"** by Willam Blake

(Use space below to have some fun continuing the parody)

"How Do I Loathe Thee" *via "How Do I Love Thee?"* *

How do I loathe thee? Let me count the ways.
I loathe thee to the depth and breadth and hollows
My soul can reach when repulsed to the limits
  of shame and disgrace.

*From **"Sonnets from the Portuguese 43: How do I love thee..."** by Elizabeth Barrett Browning

(Use space below to have some fun continuing the parody)

"Do Go Gentle Do What's Right"
via "Do Not Go Gentle Into That Good Night"*

Do go gentle, do what's right,
Dumb rage be spurned at the end of your term;
Limp, limp (if you must) but don't miss your flight.

* Poem **"Do Not Go Gentle Into That Good
Night"** by Dylan Thomas

(Use space below to have some fun continuing the parody)

"To My Detestable and Loathsome Husband" via "To My Dear and Loving Husband" *

If ever two were none, then surely we.
If ever man were loathed by wife, then thee.
If ever wife had heartache from a man,
Compare with me, ye women, if you can.

*Poem **"To My Dear and Loving Husband"**
by Anne Bradstreet

(Use space below to have some fun continuing the parody)

"(What) If ... via "If" *

(What) If you kept your head when all about you
Are using theirs to try to teach you,
(What) If you can't trust yourself when all men
    also doubt you;
But can man up and make allowance for what
    they are urging you to do...

* Poem **"If"** by Rudyard Kipling

(Use space below to have some fun continuing the parody)

A Trumpty Dumpty Retrospective

An unlikely presidential run
Down an escalator had begun
But what transpired next
Has continued to vex
The world: Against all odds, Trumpty won

There were many times we thought
Trumpty's campaign would come to naught
His ideas were hollow
We thought no one would follow
One who constantly lied – and got caught?!

There were despicable transgressions
From which he would never learn lessons
Take "Access Hollywood"
Impossible he would
Make such a revolting confession

But many such gaffes were in order
Vile comments about the border
By far the most shocking
His mimicry – mocking
A physically impaired reporter

For Trumpty nothing is out of bounds
For he and his parasitic hounds
The Senate sycophants
Like odorous house ants
All must be banned from the White House grounds

People can do that November Three
Across the nation – a voting spree
Last Limerick: One Word
VOTE! Make our voices heard
All that's at stake is Democracy!

Acknowledgements

This very necessary book would not exist anywhere but my head and on some scattered assortment of pads, notebooks, envelopes, napkins, unidentifiable scrapes of paper, margins of newspapers and magazines, bank deposit slips (very few of those), and the palm and wrist of my left hand, if not for the following group of people:

My wife, Cornelia, who is not only my best friend and unwavering supporter (no matter what!), but also the best editor for anything I write. She is precise, clear, sensitive and knows what I want to say even when I don't. Not only is her talent and reputation as a coffee aficionado legendary, Cornelia's commitment to our morning ritual to jump-start the day and get me writing is absolute.

My two sons, Nicholas and Morgan:
Nicholas knows the Trumpty territory very well, can type like a demon, and adds the eyes and vernacular of youth to keep me from lapsing into "geezer-speak." Morgan remotely, provided instant (comprehensible) answers to any tech questions, and has the POV of the millennial crowd to keep me from becoming mawkishly partisan.

Evelyn Augusto – talented poet, longtime dear friend, and a relentless supporter of this project.

Despite a hectic schedule, balancing work, family, and weekly travel throughout three different states, she made time to do research and offer feedback.

My compadre, Nick Kourabas, for our extended discussions, and his encyclopedic knowledge of the political background of those I hoped to skewer in this book. His discretion often tempered my overzealousness.

Deborah MunGavin, – poet and visual artist, and an uncommonly simpatico spirit, has an extraordinary ear for rhythm, meter, the nuances of sounds and meanings, as well as the unique ability to see how specific words, lines, and verses fit together (or not), and how they complement each other. Doesn't skimp or fail to notice one out of place word.

Jon Alderfer for his second perfect cover illustration! He is too decent a human being to not be a "typical temperamental artist…" but as his illustrations have revealed, Jon is anything but typical!

There are no words to describe the contributions of my good (and patient) pal, Dave Voytek. Dave extracted me numerous times from the stranglehold of technology, for whom I am a predictable but unwilling victim. He is the magician who made the techno-moron part of me disappear… a trick he repeated over and over again in front of my eyes and I still couldn't figure out how he did it?!

Deborah Gorman and Lee Gorman... 50 years out of college and still my closest pair of friends who are not blood relatives. They opened up their home and generosity to me for several days so that I could work uninterrupted on this book during the final critical juncture of home stretch and fatigue. I was nurtured and fed like a spoiled prince. That, in and of itself, would have been enough, but Debby's depth as a literary analyst who proofread, edited, organized, took apart, and reassembled the text while, simultaneously, refocusing yours truly – a poster model for A.D.D. – was daunting! Lee's gifts as an artist, designer, and marketing wizard cannot be overemphasized. He has forgotten more than other professionals in his field ever knew, and he works so quickly, it's impossible to determine how he arrives at what ultimately ends up on the page. One doesn't have to know any of that to appreciate the results Simply put: "No Lee = No book."

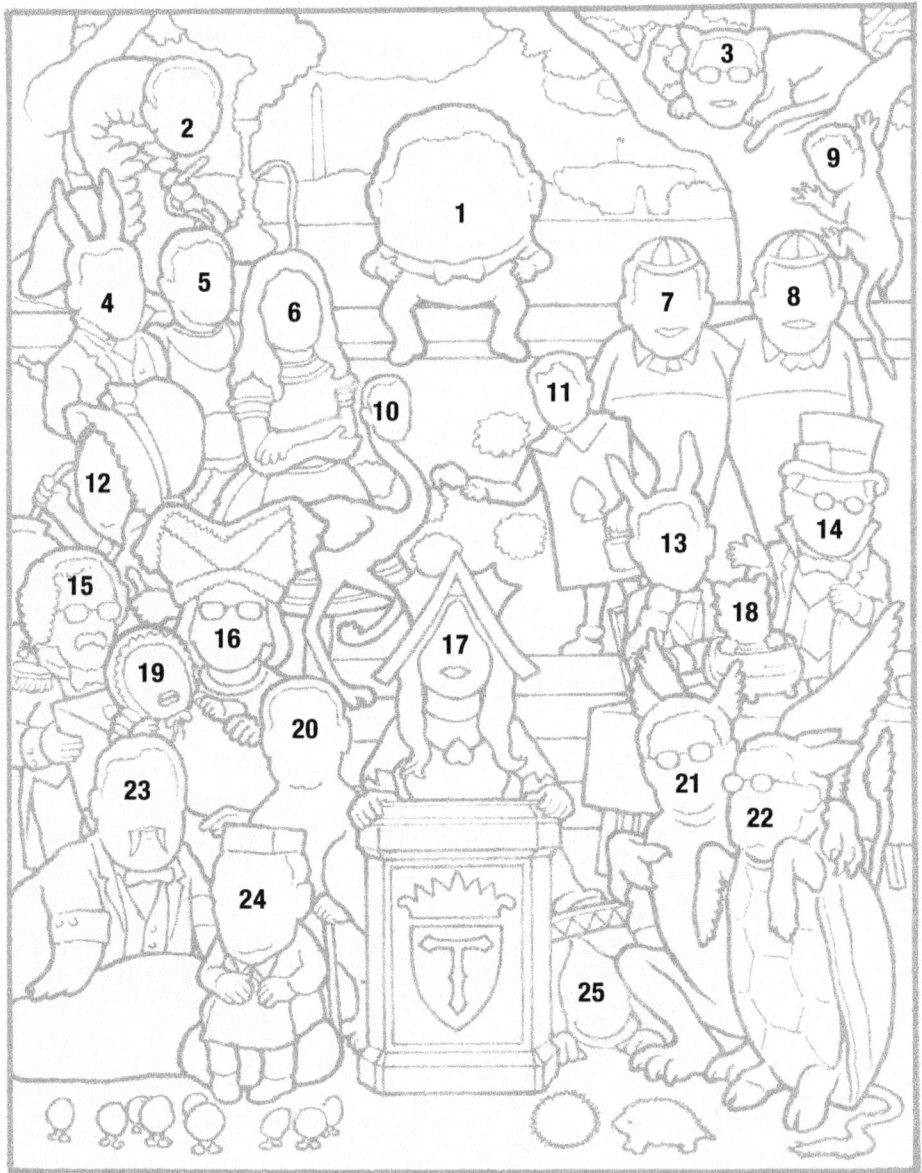

Legend

1   TRUMPTY DUMPTY

2   PUTIN   The CATERPILLAR

3   MNUCHIN   The CHESHIRE CAT

4   PENCE   The WHITE RABBIT

5   KUSHNER   The WHITE KNIGHT

6   IVANKA   ALICE

7   ERIC   TWEEDLE DEE

8   DON JR   TWEEDLE DUM

9   MANAFORT   The LIZARD

10   MILLER   The FLAMINGO

11   HANNITY   The PLAYING CARD (PLAYER)

12   SANDERS   The COOK

13   FLYNN   The MARCH HARE

14   STONE   The MAD HATTER

15   BOLTON   The ROYAL MESSENGER

16   DEVOS   The DUCHESS

17   MELANIA   The RED QUEEN

18   COHEN   The DOORMOUSE

19   GRAHAM   The PIG BABY

20   POMPEO   The DODO

21   BARR   The GRYPHON

22   McCONNELL   The MOCK TURTLE

23   CHRISTIE   The WALRUS

24   GIULIANI   The CARPENTER

25   KELLYANN   The KNAVE

www.ingramcontent.com/pod-product-compliance
Lightning Source LLC
LaVergne TN
LVHW091206080426
835509LV00006B/860